The Spinning
Study Guide 2021

CRACK THE COMPARATIVE #6

Amy Farrell

SCENE BY SCENE

WICKLOW, IRELAND

Scene by Scene
Wicklow, Ireland.
www.scenebyscene.ie

The Spinning Heart Study Guide 2021 by Amy Farrell.
ISBN 978-1-910949-83-2

Illustration © Polinaraulina

Contents

About This Book

This book is a study guide for Leaving Certificate English students sitting their exam in 2021. It provides notes for the Comparative Study of *The Spinning Heart* by Donal Ryan.

There are notes and analysis of key moments for Cultural Context/Social Setting, General Vision and Viewpoint, Relationships.

I have selected key moments to analyse for each comparative study mode. However, my choices are not definitive - any moment can be considered and explored for any mode. Feel free to consider other moments to add to your analysis for the comparative study.

'The Spinning Heart' by Donal Ryan

'The Spinning Heart' is set in a rural town following Ireland's financial collapse. The narrative centres on the protagonist, Bobby Mahon, and his troubled relationship with his father.

Notes on Cultural Context/Social Setting

This story is set within the timeframe of the recent **recession** in Ireland, the period following the **economic collapse** that occurred in 2008. Characters are out of work, with little money or job prospects. This **unemployment** leaves characters feeling ashamed and **frustrated**, and creates an environment where those with work are told to consider themselves lucky to have a job at all.

There is a culture within this world of **men repressing their emotions**, and **reacting explosively when angered**. This takes it toll on the men in the story; Seanie Shaper suffers with depression without reaching out for help, unable to articulate how is feeling. Similarly, Bobby cannot talk to Triona about what is going on when he is released on bail. **Men suffer in silence** in this society that encourages the repression of men's emotions.

Women in this text are generally wives and mothers, conforming to society's roles for them.

Women also tend to be reduced to sexual objects by the men of this world, described in terms of attractiveness and spoken of in relation to sex.

This **sexist outlook** crops up in many chapters: Seanie's, Jason's, Brian's and Rory's for example, suggesting it is widespread in this world.

This is a **violent place**. Jason recounts a shooting, Vasya remembers his brother being beaten to death, and Frank Mahon is killed in his home.

Dylan's abduction adds to the impression that this is an **unpredictable, dangerous place**. Millicent's fear of the Children Snatcher Monster shows the threat the kidnapping represents in this world, where **adults cannot keep children safe**.

There is also a certain **traditional** outlook here, as many characters' parents also lived their whole lives here. This helps create the impression that this is a **close knit community**, where people are well known to one another.

There is a downside to this close knit community. This small town is rife with **gossip, rumour and judgement**. Bobby is rumoured to be having sex with Réaltín because he visits her house to do repair work. He is also assumed to be his father's killer as their terrible relationship is well known. **This is a place where people are quick to jump to conclusions and assume the worst of each other**.

There are also positives to this small town life though. Bridie recounts taking in Bobby and his mother when Frank drunkenly smashed up their home. Her kindness and compassion shows that **goodness and understanding** are also to be found in this place.

There are many **religious** references throughout the text, which shows that religion is very much a part of these people's lives, their culture and this **traditional rural world**. The parish priest is mentioned a number of times, and Frank's chapter ends with him wondering how he will look upon the face of God, making his religious belief very clear. However, this religious aspect of their world does not appear to temper characters' actions or make them any kinder towards one another.

Cultural Context/Social Setting Key Moments

Pokey Burke Cheats His Workers

The opening chapter details the impact of the **financial collapse** in Ireland.

Bobby recalls how Pokey Burke "shafted" the men who worked for him. Mickey Briars realised that they were not in a proper pension, and violently challenged Pokey about it, demanding his pension and stamps. This moment shows how Pokey, as their boss, has **swindled the men** who work for him, abusing their trust to save himself money.

Unable to get his hands on Pokey, **Mickey cannot contain his rage and explodes in anger, violently striking Timmy with a shovel. This shows the violent behaviour of men in this world, and how the innocent are collateral damage, victims of uncontrolled anger.**

Bobby remarks that Timmy's injuries do not really matter as you don't need brains to toil on a site and take orders from men who will trick you. This is **not a world where you need to be clever, but one where you need to endure.**

Bobby describes the building site as a **harsh, difficult place** to work, and shows how Pokey has cheated the men who work for him. The **workers**

are left with nothing now that they have lost their jobs. **They have no work, no work prospects, and no social welfare payments.**

Lily is Beaten by her Baby's Father

Lily relates being beaten by the father of her baby. While in labour, Lily named the father of her fifth child. **Bernie, outraged to be named as the father of a prostitute's baby, unleashes his anger,** punching her in the mouth and saying he should kill her.

This moment shows the **violence of this world,** where Bernie channels his anger into beating Lily. **His outrage is noteworthy, he resents being known as the baby's father, this slur on his reputation maddens him and provokes this violent assault.**

This attack also shows **how little Lily is worth in this society,** how the **label of prostitute degrades her** and makes Bernie feel that he can treat her like this.

He shows no interest in his child, not wanting anything to do with them. In this world, **Bernie chooses to ignore his unwanted baby.**

The local garda sergeant is relieved when Lily says her injuries are the result of a fall, not wanting to have to follow up on her assault. **Bernie will not be held to account for this assault.**

Lily is scorned and held in disdain in this world. **Her lifetime of sex work makes her vulnerable and isolated.** Now, as an older woman she is entirely alone, forgotten by even her own children, such is their **shame.**

The **judgemental tendencies of this society are clear** in this chapter. Lily is scorned because she has spent her life selling sex to men. She is an unwanted part of the community, someone they would rather ignore.

She is a victim of **judgement and violence** in this place that refuses to acknowledge her.

Réaltín Lives in a Ghost Estate

Réaltín's home in a ghost estate perfectly captures the economic collapse of the recession. Réaltín and her neighbour are isolated and cut-off, living in an estate that was never completed.

The **other houses are unfinished and vacant, demonstrating the sudden financial ruin of the recession.**

Réaltín remembers buying her house and gives us an insight into how **misleading and untruthful** people in this world can be. The auctioneer made Réaltín and her father feel pressure to buy immediately, and that is what they did, eager to secure a home for Réaltín.

Réaltín explains that work ceased on her estate when the builder went bust. She tells us of Pokey Burke, showing how many people in this community were affected by his actions.

These days Réaltín's father cuts the grass and tidies up, **trying to maintain the facade of normalcy.** His love and affection for his daughter are clear. His relationship with his daughter and grandson show that **family love can be strong and positive in this world.**

Réaltín's relationship with Seanie, her son Dylan's father, also gives an insight into this world. Réaltín finds Seanie lacking, saying all he is good for is drinking and shagging floozies. She highlights the **drinking culture** and acceptance of **casual sex** in this world.

Réaltín is not sure if Seanie is Dylan's father, having once had sex with her boss, George. George arranged a night out, hoping that if a girl from the office had enough to drink, she might find him attractive. There is something **predatory** in George's attempts to get young female colleagues drunk and engage them sexually, suggesting a **sexist society**.

Réaltín explains how confused she was during the time she became pregnant by speaking of her mother's death, and her difficulty grieving. Like others in this world, **Réaltín carries a private pain and suffering she does not share with others, that has major impacts on her life and happiness**.

Jason - A Victim of Violence and Abuse

Jason's account shows the **difficult, harsh side of living in this world**. He has **a son he never sees** with a woman who has no interest in him.

Jason was abused as a child and has never recovered. He has suffered **trauma** ever since, which has affected his ability to function in society. Jason's story tells us that **children are not safe from predators in this world**.

He also shows how he does not fit into society because of his mental health problems, listing an array of diagnoses he suffers from that he uses to avoid job interviews.

The **violence and unpredictability** of this world is seen when he describes witnessing a shooting. **Jason is a victim of this violent world, his exposure to violence and abuse has impaired his ability to function fully in society**.

This account highlights the **sexism** of this world. Jason speaks about the tattoo artist's assistant as if she is an object, existing for men to look at. He also comments that the apartments given to "slappers" are very nice, using **derogatory language to describe single mothers**.

His own violent tendencies are seen when he says he should have assaulted his son's mother. **Jason, a victim of violence and abuse, is himself violent and abusive in his treatment of others. This suggests a difficult, dangerous world, where characters are unhappy and quick to lash out.**

Seanie's Sexism, Toxic Masculinity and Depression

Seanie's chapter shows us his **sexist views towards women** and the **effects of the culture of toxic masculinity in his society.** He suffers his depression alone, **unable to express how he feels**, his sadness, or his feelings of inadequacy.

Seanie recalls the first time he saw Réaltín. The way she looked at him made him realise how it felt for girls to be ogled and laughed and whistled at by Seanie and his friends. His comment reveals the **casual sexism** of this world and the **toxic masculinity** of Seanie and his co-workers.

Seanie tells us the whole village heard that Bobby was having an affair with Réaltín, showing how **rumour and gossip** are rife in this small, rural community.

Seanie mentions how his family keep secrets out of embarrassment, not wanting to speak about themselves for fear of being judged or looking foolish. He reveals how his culture makes it difficult for him to be open and honest, how **there is a focus on being closed and keeping things to** oneself.

Seanie struggles with his depression alone. He describes how his life has disappointed him, how things have not turned out as he hoped, and how he struggles with this. He **keeps his depression a secret** and cannot bring himself to speak of it. **In this world he cannot be open about his mental health problems.** He allows others to think he is carefree, when in reality he is troubled and depressed. **Seanie secretly suffers his depression, unable to express how he feels in this society.**

Seanie's feelings of inadequacy cause problems in his relationship with Réaltín. He gets mean and nasty with her and cannot express how he wants things to be. He feels that she wants him to be a proper man, and that he falls short. **The emphasis on this macho idea of masculinity is problematic**, it is an ideal Seanie does not feel he can live up to. The pressure he feels leads to him lashing out at Réaltín; **in this world, women are the targets of men's anger.**

Denis' Financial Desperation and Violence

Denis' chapter reveals the pressure and violence of this world in extensive detail. He appears as an isolated figure, suffering from **incredible stress** because of his **dire financial situation.** He is **heavily in debt** and cannot collect what is owed to him, while his wife is only barely tolerating him. Denis is frustrated by his inability to collect the money that he is due, and **his stress and frustration is converted to rage** without any other outlet for it. He talks about driving around the country looking for the men that owe him nearly a hundred grand. He did four or five jobs that he was never paid anything for, and this predicament gives an insight into how **severely he has been affected by the collapse of the building trade.**

Denis speaks of nearly driving over a man in Lackagh, and nearly going through a plate-glass office door in Galway to reach a man who was avoiding him. **In this world it seems, resorting to violence is a response for angry men**.

Denis describes how imagining himself hitting his wife was the only thing that stopped him from actually hitting her.

Denis' search for a link to Pokey Burke, for someone responsible for his situation, is what leads him to Frank Mahon's house. He wanted to scare the old man and make him feel bad about his son, Pokey's foreman. Once again, **in this place, bad feeling and hurt leads to further destruction and suffering**.

Denis bludgeoned Frank Mahon with a length of wood, imagining himself killing his own father as he did so. In this way **Denis highlights a number of aspects of this world, its violence, the frustration and lack of control characters feel due to their economic situation, and the disastrous relationships so many have with their fathers**.

Denis' chapter ends with him alone, curled up in bed, tormented by what he has done. His sorrowful state shows us that **despite the violence of this world,** these flawed characters are very emotional and human.

Notes on General Vision and Viewpoint

In this novel, the author offers an **outlook** where **life is overwhelmingly full of difficulty, suffering and sadness.**

The collapse of the economy has resulted in financial difficulty for the novel's characters, with some feeling pushed to emigrate as **life at home feels empty of prospects.** Financial pressure makes characters like Rory feel he cannot participate in a social life, while Denis' money problems lead to extreme **stress and violence.**

It is not just the recession that makes characters feel trapped and hopeless however. Each character recounts how they have **suffered loss and grief** in their lives. There are stories of **rejection, death, loneliness, depression, fear and an inability to reach out to others, ask for help or express personal sorrows.** Added to this are those with mental health issues and depression. **The novel shows us how dark life can be.**

Overall, the mood of the novel is one of **sadness.** Each chapter reveals the **losses and disappointments** of a lifetime, and tells of how characters have been hurt and have suffered. **Negative, traumatising relationships** and **grief** surface repeatedly, creating a sense of **pain and sorrow.** Characters have suffered in life, some are broken by their experiences and are trapped in their sadness.

The death of Bridie's son and Vasya's brother shows that **we cannot keep those we love safe in this life, a terrifying and dark thought. Life is trying and dangerous,** something further compounded by the kidnapping and murder plotlines. **Frightening and upsetting things happen, which scar and wound characters, presenting a dark view of life.**

While the **outlook is consistently bleak, life is not shown to be without hope.** Although many characters suffer grief and sadness, their emotion shows them to be vulnerable, human people. This vulnerability shows their humanity. This is **a harsh world, but it not a cold or unfeeling one.**

Characters care deeply about one another, even if they find it difficult to express their feelings. There is **warmth** in Réaltín's **love** for her father and son, and in Bobby's devotion to Triona and her unfailing love for him. **Their loving, supportive relationship and the way they value each other offers hope and positivity in this otherwise bleak world**. Love is shown to be a powerful and redemptive force, offering characters solace and happiness. The reader gets the sense that together, Triona and Bobby will be okay, a **hopeful and forward-looking outlook**.

General Vision and Viewpoint
Key Moments

Bobby's Struggles

Bobby's account shows **how hard and trying life can be**. His **life is full of difficulty** and despair. He finds himself unemployed and experiencing **feelings of shame and inadequacy**. His joblessness makes him feel **insecure, adrift and fearful**, creating a **grim outlook** and adding a sense of **despondency about life**.

His relationship with his father is fraught. Bobby feels responsible for his father, visiting him daily, but he hates this man whose **cruel behaviour has scarred him**.

He describes how his father destroyed Bobby's bond with his mother. Bobby and his mother were afraid to speak around his father for **fear** of his sharp tongue and bitter words. Now that his mother has died, Bobby is **filled with regret and remorse** that he cannot go back and enjoy his relationship with her. **She is lost to him forever**, a sad truth which causes him much **grief** and sorrow.

Bobby's account, though saddening and sorrowful, is not entirely dark. Bobby has positives and hope in his life. He speaks highly of his wife Triona, showing the significance of **love**. He also **looks to the future** and hopes for improvements in his work situation.

His efforts to find work, his resilience, determination and sincere love for his wife suggest that although life is harsh and difficult, it is not without its rewards. Bobby has suffered, but his striving is not in vain, there is hope for the future.

Lily is Scorned and Forgotten

Lily is a figure of **shame** in her community. As a sex worker **she is an outcast, rejected even by her children.** Her chapter highlights **how harsh life can be, how somebody can be reduced to nothing by society's judgements and prejudices.** Lily is an embarrassment to her community, a figure to be condemned, showing the **cold side of human nature** and the trying, difficult side of human life.

Lily speaks of being beaten by the father of her fifth baby. He was moved to **rage and violence** such was his outrage at being named as the father of her child. This man, who she loved, repays her with a vicious beating and never shows any interest in his child. Here, the author shows **how cruel and unkind life can be.**

Lily's life has been hard, and now, as an older woman, she is entirely alone. Her children are ashamed of her, and do not visit. There is the sense that **life has treated Lily unfairly. She is forgotten by the men who once visited her, and scorned by her own children. She reminds us of how hard life can be, how isolating and judgemental our world is to**

outcasts and outsiders.

Jason Catalogues his Problems

Jason's chapter opens with the news of Frank Mahon's **murder**, setting the tone for a **depiction of life as unpredictable, violent and cruel**. Jason speaks of the **traumas** he has suffered in life and demonstrates how he has been **affected by these hardships**. **He cannot function in society, he is scarred and broken by his life's experiences, a troubling and saddening reality.**

Adding to his situation is his own poor judgment. He tells us he **regrets** getting tattoos all over his face. His regret and unhappiness with himself adds to the **feeling of dissatisfaction and gloom** in this chapter.

Jason got his tattoos to impress a woman who dropped him once he got her pregnant. **He has only seen his son once, another sad aspect to his story.**

Jason tells us he is a dependent adult child, **a victim of childhood sexual abuse**. This **abuse has damaged Jason**, making him unable to lead a regular, independent adult life. He lists a litany of conditions he suffers from, a list he learned off by heart to avoid job interviews. **Jason believes he is damaged and broken** and appears to resent the authority of those in the job centre, further creating the sense that **he has opted out of life as it has been so hard on him.**

He tells us he got **post-traumatic shock after witnessing a shooting**. For Jason, **life has been especially frightening and unkind**. In his account, Jason catalogues his unhappiness, his lack of joy or love. **His voice darkens the outlook, presenting life as a series of trials and challenges for him to fail**. The outlook here is **bleak**, without much hope or light.

However, this chapter is not totally hopeless. Jason speaks highly of Bobby Mahon, recognising the **kindness** in him when he gave Jason's father a new wheel for his car. **Bobby's generosity shows that warmth in humanity is always possible.**

Millicent's Unhappy Home

Millicent's chapter gives an insight into what it is like to be a child in this world. Talking about her parents, she describes a **dysfunctional, unhappy marriage.** Millicent's mother is frustrated with her father's joblessness, and **she vents her anger at him, calling him useless** and a bad example.

Millicent does not understand a lot of what is said in her house, but her responses to what is going on around her adds to the story's outlook and the author's view of life. **The stress and strain of modern life is clear.**

She cried when she heard her mother say that she works her fingers to the bone in Tescos and describes **crying at dinner without knowing why. Her emotional upset suggests not just sadness, but stress and confusion. She does not understand her life, but is upset and distressed by it.**

She realises that her father is unhappy and is sad when her mother is around. Millicent does not want to go to school in September as she does not want her daddy to be sad without her. **Her attachment to her father shows warmth and positivity, but his situation is quite bleak.** He is without work, or the prospect of work, a situation that is causing much strife in his marriage.

Millicent's parents' fears about the Children Snatcher Monster creates the sense that life is dangerous and unpredictable. Her mother's response to hearing of the snatched child is to accuse Hughie of not looking after Millicent properly. Hughie gets very upset and he and his wife comfort each other.

Although their relationship is fraught and problematic, here we see compassion and warmth. Their lives are difficult and their relationship is under great strain, but moments of love and positivity remain. The outlook, though dark, is not completely bleak.

The chapter ends with Millicent lying in bed, unable to sleep for fear of the Children Snatcher Monster and afraid to call her parents in case it causes a row. Her perspective shows us **how frightening and uncertain life can be. She is scared and afraid, unable to ask her parents to comfort her.** Her account shows how trying, difficult and frightening life can be.

Frank's Bitterness

Frank's chapter tells a story of **the damaging effects of violence and abuse and their impact on family relationships.** He creates the impression that **life is full of suffering and hardship, inevitable consequences of living.** His life shows **the strangling effect of bitterness on love**, how his mean-spirited ways crushed his family and starved them of love and affection.

His opening words speak of the future as a cold mistress. **Hope has always proved false for Frank, life has been cold and disappointing** and his violent murder does not seem to surprise him.

When Bobby discovered Frank's body, Frank told his son he was a good man. It is sad that Frank only spoke these words after his death. He goes on to describe Bobby as being without a dust of sense. **His words against his son grate in this chapter**. The reader is saddened to see Frank speak poorly of his own son, who others have praised throughout the novel.

He goes on to speak about his wife, saying she always felt she was better than him. **Frank's attitude towards his wife and son cost him dearly. His coldness and disregard is saddening, painting a bleak picture of life where relationships bring suffering rather than warmth or support**. He is aware of how he cut his wife and son with his words, a failing he could not control.

Frank goes on to describe being **savagely beaten by his father as a boy**. He had rushed to tell his father of how clever he was in school, but his pride earned him not praise, but violence and cruelty. This episode helps the reader to understand Frank. He became bitter and cruel because of his father.

He describes doing violence to things, imagining himself killing his father. **The overwhelming sense here is of waste and loss, Frank has suffered and caused suffering, and for what? The outlook is grim and dispiriting, a life wasted for nothing.**

Triona's Love for Bobby & Dylan's Safety

The bleakness and sadness of the novel is not absolute. In the final chapter, Triona speaks of her **love for and belief in Bobby**, reaffirming the reader's belief in him as a good man. Triona truly knows and understands her husband, and loves him for who he is, **a very positive aspect to the novel's outlook**.

Her account shows **life's hardships**. She speaks of her cousin, Coley, who took his own life at fourteen, and describes Bobby as barely surviving his father. Triona shows great **understanding and compassion** in her account; she reminds us of **how warm and supportive people can be**.

Triona does not care if Bobby never earned another cent, nor would she care if Bobby had killed his father. Her **unwavering love is very affirming and positive. She reminds us that love is possible.**

Her account is a mix of sadness and hope. While she loves and values Bobby, she resents Frank, and is angry that he lived while her own lovely father died. She has also **experienced life's pain and sorrows**.

She speaks of the gleeful way that locals gossip, thriving on bad news and speculation. This, coupled with her words about Frank's spiteful ways shows that **people can be cruel and judgemental. She draws attention to both the good and bad in people and how this impacts on our lives**.

Another significant aspect of Triona's chapter is that she tells us that **the kidnapped child has been found alive and well**. Jim Gildea, the sergeant, walked in and retrieved him without any use of force. This act of **redemption** brings **relief** to the reader; **a terrible outcome has been averted, the boy has been saved and good has triumphed. This story strand has a happy ending.**

As Triona looks to the future, there is a sense of **hope and optimism** that has been largely absent from the novel. Triona, as the final speaker, **ends the story on a hopeful note**. Her compassion and love, coupled with the safety of the kidnapped boy, makes this **an uplifting moment** in the story. **This is a positive episode in what has been a very emotional and saddening narrative.**

Notes on Theme/Issue - Relationships

The relationships portrayed in this novel are overwhelmingly negative, destructive and saddening. Few characters, with the exception of Bobby and Triona, experience real love, warmth or support in their lives, but rather are crippled by the effects of damaging relationships. This is a central theme in the novel, **showing the unhappiness that poor relationships can cause in characters' lives.**

Frank Mahon has treated Bobby and his mother with **spite and scorn** throughout his life, eroding their bond as they were afraid to speak around him for fear of accusations and his sharp tongue.

Both as a child and now as an adult, Bobby's relationship with his father is extremely flawed. Bobby visits his father every day. Physically, Bobby is present in his father's life, but this is **a shell of a relationship, empty of warmth or love**. In fact, even in death, Frank mocks and belittles Bobby, forever seeing his son's failings.

Frank himself was the victim of an abusive father, who once beat him severely with a length of wavin pipe for boasting about being clever in school. This shows the **prevalence of anger and violence** in the relationships in the story.

There is a sense of inevitablity surrounding these relationships, they are doomed to fail and cause misery and unhappiness.

Bobby's negative relationship with his father is magnified and amplified by other similar father-son relationships in the text. Denis also speaks of hating his father, while Timmy's father was completely absent, abandoning him and his siblings. **Sons hating their fathers is a**

recurring idea. Frank's murder powerfully demonstrates this theme; Bobby is suspected, as their failed relationship and Frank's vicious nature are so well known, but it was actually another man who hated his father that killed Frank. This shows **how common these failed relationships are**, and also **how damaging their effects can be**.

Even when relationships are not marked by violence, many bring sorrow and disappointment to characters' lives, and many experience **loneliness and isolation.** Bridie is a very lonely character, forever affected by her son's drowning, which led to the breakdown of her marriage. Seanie Shaper is similarly alone, feeling inadequate and adrift after his failed relationship with Réaltín. **Characters struggle with their relationships, hampered by their inability to express themselves emotionally** and really say what is in their hearts.

In this way, **an inability to communicate** is seen to be a common trait in many of these relationships, just as **violence** is. In both cases, these **flaws erode and break down relationships, making characters unhappy**.

A redeeming, positive relationship we see is that of Bobby and Triona. Bobby loves his wife, just as she loves him. They offer a glimpse of warmth, support and positive emotion that is absent from many of the other relationships in the novel. Threats to their marriage, such as Réaltín's pursuit of Bobby, the rumours that arise regarding Bobby and Réaltín, and the murder charge, are all insignificant by the novel's end, suggesting a strong, committed, loving relationship.

There are **also positive family relationships,** such as Réaltín and her kind, considerate father, and Rory and his respect for his parents.

However, these positive relationships do not bring balance to the theme. Overall, the sense is that relationships in the story are

generally negative (overwhelmingly so in places), and they bring sorrow and difficulty to characters' lives.

Theme/Issue - Relationships
Key Moments

Bobby's Hatred for his Father (Frank)

The novel's opening paragraph details how Bobby and his spiteful father feel about one another. **Bobby and his father, Frank, have a very negative relationship.**

Bobby tells us that **Frank always found fault** in his son and wife. His account of living with his father shows how bitter and spiteful the older man was and how he lashed out and hurt those around him with his actions and sharp words.

Frank found fault in everything, making Bobby and his mother afraid to do anything or speak freely in front of him. In this way, Frank not only ruined his own relationship with his wife and son, but destroyed the bond between them too, something that fills Bobby with **regret**. Bobby cannot go back and put things right with his mother, her death prevents him from mending their relationship.

Bobby carries a burden of hatred towards his father, resenting him for destroying his bond with his mother. Bobby tells us at the beginning of the novel that he visits his father each day in the hope of finding him dead, a truth that highlights the **bad feeling** he harbours towards him.

He then goes on to tell us that **he imagines killing his father**, picturing himself suffocating the old man. **Bobby wishes for his father's death, giving an insight into how much he despises him, how damaged and dysfunctional their relationship is.**

The lasting impression of Bobby's troubled relationship with his father is that of hatred and waste. They are tied together by pain and resentment in a toxic bond that brings only pain. It is worth noting how this negative relationship has impacted on Bobby, causing him sadness, loss and regret.

Jason's Relationship with the Mother of his Child

Jason's account is marked by **negative relationships** and damaging experiences, adding to the negative portrayal of relationships in the text.

Jason tells us matter of factly that Bobby Mahon killed his father. As his account unfolds it seems that **negative relationships and violence are the norm** in his life.

He says the biggest mistake he made was getting tattoos all over his face, something he did for a woman. He says he would have done anything she wanted, and acted on her suggestion to get a spider tattooed on his cheek.

Jason sounds young and vulnerable as he describes how this girl wanted to get pregnant by him, and then wanted him for little else. Jason says he **only saw his son once**. He clearly **feels rejected** by this girl whose child he fathered.

She wants nothing to do with him, and his lack of contact with his son causes him unhappiness. **Jason too is a victim of negative relationships**. He deals poorly with his sadness and feelings of rejection. He tells us that he should have burst through the door and slapped the head off his son's mother when she would not let him into her home to see his son. **Like other frustrated, angry characters in the novel, he feels resorting to violence is the way to get what he want**s.

Jason is a victim of sexual abuse, violence and destructive relationships, and has been traumatised and damaged by his experiences, contributing to his inability to function properly in society. He mentions many interactions and **relationships that damaged him** in some way: the girl who only wanted to get pregnant and then cut him out of her life, the neighbour who sexually abused him, the culchie who shot someone in front of him. **Jason's account highlights the damaging effect of destructive relationships and the huge impact they have on those subjected to them**.

Denis and Kate's Loveless Marriage

Denis and Kate's marriage appears to lack love and understanding. As his chapter begins, Denis is curled up in the foetal position, lying in bed for days. His wife offers him no comfort though, he says she is only **barely tolerating him** and is very close to telling him to cop on and pull himself together. He realises how his wife feels about him, and the disdain she holds him in. There is **no warmth or concern** on Kate's part, Denis appears to be suffering alone.

Denis does not seem to feel positively towards his wife either. **His money troubles have added stress and anxiety to his relationship** with Kate, making them **at odds with one another**. He describes picturing himself giving Kate a punch in the mouth, saying imagining this violence was the only way he could stop himself from actually doing it. This **violence and anger directed towards his wife** suggests a serious flaw in their relationship.

Denis goes on to say that **Kate does not know him**, or his thoughts. She does not realise that he is filled with rage, or that he feels so violently towards her. This **gulf between them**, this lack of understanding, is a **negative comment on their marriage**, just as Denis' violent feelings are.

By the end of his chapter it seems that Kate does not know that Denis has killed a man. He hides his crime from her. Denis is suggesting that **his wife does not know the man she is married to** at all, a very negative comment on their relationship. It also adds to the sense that he is very **isolated and cut-off**, dealing with his fears and guilt entirely **alone**.

Mags is Shamed by her Father (Josie)

Mags and her father have a relationship that **lacks closeness or understanding**. She describes how **distant** they are with one another, a gap that cannot be closed.

She imagines sneaking out to listen to him talking to his chickens, knowing that this would embarrass him and that he would be unable to talk to her about it. **She imagines a better version of their relationship**, one where he could put his arm around her and chat to her the way he does with his son and niece and nephew, knowing this can never be the case.

Mags recounts being **ridiculed by her father** at a dinner party. He can no longer love her as he once did. Now that he knows she is a lesbian **he feels ashamed of her**. His prejudice and lack of understanding hinders Josie's ability to treat his daughter as she needs him to, leading to a **disintegration of their once loving bond**.

At this moment, when he hurts her most, Mags wishes for the father from her youth to kiss her forehead and brush her hair back from her forehead. There is sadness in this fond memory, and in **Josie's inability to be the loving father that Mags needs**.

He cannot accept her and love her, caught up in his own prejudices and homophobia. This is another example of **a flawed relationship that causes unhappiness**, adding to the theme of **damaged and hurtful relationships, where those that should love most, deeply fail their loved ones**. Josies lets Mags down when he shames her in front of guests and fails to be the father that she needs. She closes her chapter wishing that he could remember how he loved her, clinging to the memory of her loving father from childhood.

Frank Mahon Remembers Being Beaten by his Father

Frank Mahon's account of being viciously assaulted by his father sheds some light on his character and relationships with his family. It seems that **Frank was himself a victim of violence and cruelty**, something he never managed to overcome, becoming in time a version of his own cruel, hurtful father. **He is a product of destructive relationships**, sadly continuing this cycle of anger and hurt.

Frank relates how he was beaten with a length of wavin piping by his father as a boy. He rushed into the milking parlour to tell his father how clever he was in school, but instead of praise, Frank received a beating. He had got every question right while the cigire visited his school, something his teacher was delighted about. However, instead of taking pride in his son, Frank's father is enraged. He beats the boy with the piping, knocking him flat onto the mucky ground and shouting at him that he knows nothing.

Frank's youthful pride and innocence was met with violence and cruelty, an episode that had a lasting effect on Frank and contributed to his hatred of his father. **This moment in the story showcases negative relationships and their lasting impact, showing how the abuse Frank suffered helped shape his own destructive relationships with others**. This moment also adds to the idea of **negative father-son relationships** and how harmful these relationships can be.

During his drinking days, **Frank used to imagine himself strangling his father**, choking the life from him. These **violent, emotional images** add to our understanding of the force of his **hatred for his father** and this destructive, hateful relationship.

Frank's recollection of being beaten by his father brings the issue of negative relationships to the fore. It shows how negative relationships affect characters and hinder their ability to be happy and forge positive relationships of their own.

Triona's Love for Bobby

Triona's view of Bobby and the love she has for him show a very positive side to relationships in the novel. Triona loves Bobby and admires who he is.

Triona remembers the first time she spoke to Bobby, and how from that moment on she was wrapped up in him. Her certainty and devotion here are very positive, showing how strongly she feels about him. This **depth of steadfast feeling is a feature of their marriage**. In the Cave bar Triona became aware of Bobby's fear, doubt, shyness and sadness. **Her deep understanding of Bobby and her total acceptance of him are very positive aspects of their relationship.**

Triona's love for Bobby is unconditional. She tells us she would not care if he never earned another penny, his traditional role of provider is not important to her. She also does not care about the rumours about Bobby having an affair, knowing that he would never betray her. Triona has **complete faith** in her husband.

Triona goes on to say that she would not care if Bobby had killed his father. There is no judgement here, just love and support.

Her chapter matches Bobby's earlier one in the positive way she speaks about her spouse, **their marriage demonstrates mutual love, understanding and support**, and their **commitment** to each other and **certainty of their love** makes it the **most positive relationship in the text**.

Triona understands how Bobby has been hurt by his father, her compassion is a positive aspect of their relationship.

However, **their marriage is not perfect**. It is marred by **Bobby's inability to communicate freely and openly** with Triona.

Bobby cannot speak openly to Triona when he is released on bail. She screams at him to please talk to her. **An inability to communicate openly is a flaw in their marriage, but it does not lessen Triona's love for her husband**. Like the novel's other relationships, theirs is **complex and complicated**, but here we see real **love and understanding** without a shadow of the bitterness and hate of so many other relationships in the text.

9 781910 949832